The 17.6 Year
Stock Market Cycle

Connecting the Panics of 1929, 1987, 2000 and 2007

Kerry Balenthiran

HARRIMAN HOUSE LTD

3A Penns Road
Petersfield
Hampshire
GU32 2EW
GREAT BRITAIN

Tel: +44 (0)1730 233870
Email: enquiries@harriman-house.com
Website: www.harriman-house.com

First published in Great Britain in 2013
Copyright © Harriman House Ltd

ISBN: 978-0857192-73-8

British Library Cataloguing in Publication Data
A CIP catalogue record for this book can be obtained from the British Library.

 Harriman House

CONTENTS

ABOUT THE AUTHOR

Kerry Balenthiran studied mathematics at the University of Warwick and then worked as a Spacecraft Operations Engineer in the UK and at the European Space Agency. He qualified as a chartered accountant with Arthur Andersen and now works as a consultant within financial services. His mathematical background led to a fascination with the cyclical nature of stock market booms and busts.

INTRODUCTION

The stock market first attracted my attention during the technology bubble crash in 2000. Everyone knew that there were no profits underpinning dotcom company valuations, but now it seemed that some of the revenues didn't exist either. A number of high profile frauds, such as Enron and WorldCom, were exposed by the 2001 recession. This was of particular interest to me because my employer at the time, Arthur Andersen, appeared to be at the centre of the accounting storm and I was facing the prospect of losing my job.

Most of my friends and colleagues were investing in the stock markets at the end of the 1990s. The fact that they knew nothing about investing didn't bother them, whatever they bought went up in price and therefore it was an easy way to make money. As far as they were concerned they couldn't go wrong.

My future wife and I saved up and bought our first house instead. All of my friends told me that this wasn't a good use of my money, house prices wouldn't rise as they had done in the past, the 1980s was a one-off. I have always been an independent thinker and I was in love so I ignored them all and did what I felt was best.

In hindsight we now know that the herd mentality that was prevalent at the time of the tulip mania in 1637 and the South Sea bubble of 1720 was in full flow at the end of the 1990s. I have no idea what causes it but it was there and this behaviour recurs consistently throughout history.

In 2003 I started investing in the stock market, confident that the once in a lifetime 1929 style stock market crash was behind us and that we were entering the start of another great bull market. There was much debate about whether the subsequent rally was a bear market rally or a new bull market but this didn't concern me at the time. The market was going up and so were my investments.

In February 2007 HSBC issued a shock profits warning related to its US mortgage business and *Moneyweek* magazine was reporting that the US and UK property bubbles would burst triggering a devastating banking crisis. My understanding of the markets was still somewhat limited but I knew enough to understand that a property crash was bad for consumer spending and therefore company profits. I decided to get out of the stock market and sold all of my investments so that I could concentrate on finding out more about bear markets.

At first I intended to study economics to understand the drivers of the wider economy, however the credit crunch had me questioning the value of mainstream thinking, particularly after I read George Soros' book *The New Paradigm for Financial Markets: The Credit Crisis of 2008 and What It Means*. Soros' ability to make money from the markets, while being dismissive of economic theory on the behaviour of stock prices, convinced me that I would be better off pursuing my own independent research.

The insurance industry is acutely aware of infrequent but regular reoccurring events such as 100 year floods or 250 year earthquakes. Just because something hasn't happened in our lifetime it doesn't mean that it won't, and I set about applying this same approach to stock markets. I believe that not having an investing or economic background has helped me in my study of bear markets and cyclical nature of stock markets.

A cycle of length 17.6 years is not new

A cycle is a sequence of events that repeat over time. The outcome won't necessarily be the same each time, but the underlying characteristics are the same. A good example is the seasonal cycle. Each year we have spring, summer, autumn and winter, and after winter we have spring again. But the weather can, and does, vary a great deal from one year to another.

As you will see, the identification of a 17 to 18 year stock market cycle is nothing new; in fact a stock market cycle of length exactly 17.6 years is not new either. Art Cashin from Swiss bank UBS, interviewed on CNBC in 2009, discussed a bull market cycle (the overriding trend is up) lasting 17.6 years followed by a bear market cycle (the overriding trend is down) of 17.6 years. Cashin said that if you take the top of the bull market to be 2000, then subtracting 17.6 years gives 1982.4, the start of the bull market, and adding 17.6 years gives 2017.6, the end of this current bear market. Cashin also extrapolated the 17.6 year cycle back just as I have done. In addition to Cashin, in his book *The Great Super Cycle*, David Skarica references the work of Steven Williams of Cycle Pro Outlook who has also identified an alternating bull then bear cycle of 17.6 years using an inflation-adjusted Dow Jones Industrial Average.

What is new is that I have gone further and established not only the regular 17.6 year periodic cycle that exists in the stock market, but I have also identified the specific intermediate turning points that repeat within the 17.6 year cycle.

I have discovered a stock market cycle consisting of increments of 2.2 years that I have extrapolated back over 100 years. I have called this cycle, rather modestly (and, after all, it has to be called something), the *Balenthiran Cycle*. That is the subject of this book.

The fact that the full Balenthiran Cycle matches cycles that have already been by identified by Cashin and Williams aligns it with concepts that have already been brought into the public domain.

Shaping our understanding of the future

This book is aimed at serious investors, both professional and private. Serious investors tend to be open minded as they seek an edge that allows them to extract enhanced profits from the stock markets. The ability to anticipate the length of broad market trends and changes in the psychological mood of market participants is a clear edge that investors can profit from. In terms of seeking that edge, I have researched and provided answers to the following key questions:

- When does a bear market end?

- Was the 2009 stock market low the end of the bear market?

- When does a new bull market begin?

This book discusses the bear markets following the 1929 top, 1966 top, 2000 top and subsequent bull markets, and it illustrates the similar characteristics that all of these periods share and outlines my expectations for the remainder of the current bear market.

Whether you believe in stock market cycles or not, I'd ask you to read this book with an open mind and allow yourself to be surprised by what you read.

The purpose of looking back at the history of the stock market is to allow it to shape our understanding of the future.

CHAPTER 1

Commodity Cycles

The twentieth century saw three long commodities bulls (1906-1923, 1933-1953, 1968-1982), each lasting an average of a little more than 17 years.

Jim Rogers, *Hot Commodities*

The first time I read about market cycles was in the book *Hot Commodities* by Jim Rogers. Rogers identifies three long-term secular commodity bull markets lasting approximately 17 years. The commodity markets are currently in a bull run that started in the late 1990s. Whether the gold price peaked in a speculative bubble in September 2011 and similarly oil in June 2008 is debatable. But what is clear is that there are cycles that run through the commodity markets and these cycles have a direct impact on the stock market.

The reason for these cycles is straightforward supply and demand, as the following illustrates:

- During the 1970s the oil price spiked in 1973 and 1979 due to tension in the Middle East restricting supply and peaked at nearly $40 in 1980.

- Once supply stabilised prices fell but Western nations realised that they were over-dependant on oil-producing countries and so alternative energy sources such as nuclear were developed, further undermining prices. In addition the high prices weakened demand considerably as consumers moved towards smaller, fuel efficient cars.

- An environment of low oil prices meant that there was little incentive to invest in oil production and new technology and smaller producers/refiners exited the market by being taken over by the oil majors, concentrating supply amongst fewer companies. The oil price hit a low of around $10.

- Once again demand was surging due to a growing economy on the back of low manufacturing prices as a result of the low oil price. However, supply had been steadily declining due to a lack of investment and now oil prices started to rise.

- The oil price increased and peaked at $147 in 2008 and the resulting increase in inflation and interest rates, which reduced disposable incomes, caused homeowners to default on their mortgages and triggered the global credit crunch and subsequent recession.

Similar supply and demand and over/under investment drivers impact all commodity markets and these take many years to filter through to the point where cost effective alternative products and/or sources of supply are available and there is a demand for these alternatives.

Rogers' book discusses the commodities cycle at length and also touches on how it affects the stock market:-

> Studies have confirmed this negative correlation between stocks and stuff. Two recent studies, for example, headed by Barry Bannister, a capital-goods analyst for Stifel Nicolaus and Co., the financial services company, show that for the past 130 years "stocks and commodities have alternated leadership in regular cycles averaging 18 years."
>
> It looks as if God himself were a trader who enjoyed playing the stock market for 18 years or so and then switched to futures, until he got bored again, after another 18 years or so, and went back into the stock market.[1]

The impact of commodities on the stock market

The impact of commodities on stock markets can be thought of as follows: commodities (raw materials) are purchased by producers and manufacturers to make goods, they in turn sell to retailers and ultimately consumers. Consumers use their disposable income to consume stuff and to spend on property.

1. At the beginning of the cycle commodity supply is low; this causes commodity price inflation. Manufacturers respond by putting up prices to maintain margins. Ultimately this reduces demand as consumers have to economise. Consumer spending falls and stock markets fall.

2. The feedback mechanism causes commodity prices to fall, now manufacturers get a boost to their profit margins and company profits and stock prices rise. Competition increases and the economy grows.

3. Increased corporate profitability causes wages to increase and when combined with falling commodity prices, real disposable incomes increase.

---

[1] *Hot Commodities*, Jim Rogers.

4. The economy continues to grow, consumers buy houses or trade up and eventually consumer demand peaks. Demand exceeds supply and commodity prices rise and the whole process starts again.

To summarise, the rising commodity prices increase input costs and reduce company profits, and also consumers' disposable incomes (demand). Conversely falling commodity prices reduce input costs and boost profits and disposable incomes. As Rogers states:

> There is no mystery to it. What could be more straightforward in this world than its very basic materials? Corn is corn, lead is lead, and even gold is just another thing whose price depends on how much of the stuff is around and how eager people are to own it. And there is certainly no magic to figuring out the direction in which prices will go in the long term. These alternating long bear and bull markets in metals, hydrocarbons, livestock, grains, and other agricultural products do not fall from the sky. They are prime players in history, the offspring of the basic economic principles of supply and demand. When supplies and inventories are plentiful, prices will be low; but once supplies are allowed to become depleted and demand increases, prices will rise, just as inevitably.[2]

The existence of a commodity cycle makes sense based on supply and demand and associated over/under investment. Studies have confirmed that commodities and stocks are negatively correlated and Bannister has shown that they alternate in regular cycles averaging 18 years.

But why 18 years?

In the following chapter we'll find out about recognised business cycles of varying lengths that have been identified and the causes of these cycles. We'll then look at how these cycles impact the stock market and drive booms and busts.

---

[2] *Ibid.*

CHAPTER 2

Business Cycles –
A Historical Perspective

The disadvantage of men not knowing the past is that they do not know the present.

G. K. Chesterton

There is a tendency among people to disregard the past, a belief that the past is history and that it has no role in terms of learning about the future. Past behaviour, in terms of markets and people, can be very insightful in terms of anticipating the future course of action.

Our understanding of business cycles doesn't appear to have improved significantly since the Great Depression. Prior to 2007 there was a general complacency that the business cycle had been tamed and this complacency arguably contributed to the banking crisis.

The banking crisis of 2007/8 was by no means a one off and by looking back at history we can gain a better understanding of what causes these crises. Much of this knowledge has long since been forgotten, since banking and finance professionals from the early 1900s are no longer with us and are therefore not able to inform people today.

Before getting to the 17.6 year stock market cycle I'll explore some of the drivers of the stock market, particularly the business cycle identified by Clement Juglar and more specifically the credit cycle that was first documented by John Mills in 1867.

The term *business cycle* refers to changes in economic activity that reoccur over a number of years. A business cycle comprises periods of growth, stagnation and decline (recession). Once one business cycle ends a new period of growth emerges and the cycle continues. When Juglar first identified the business cycle he called it a fixed investment cycle, however today it is also referred to as an economic cycle.

Juglar, Mills and Kitchin

Juglar, a French physician, was the first to identify an investment cycle of prosperity, crisis and liquidation with a periodicity of between 8 and 11 years, and he believed that prosperity leads to over-speculation that leads to a crisis. This became known as the *Juglar Cycle* with an approximate length of nine years.

British businessman John Mills presented the theory that business cycles are driven by credit cycles governed by the psychological mood of the masses. Mills believed that business cycles consisted of three periods: after a panic or crisis there will be a **post panic period** of depressed trade where credit is restricted; a **revival period** where trade and employment pick up and credit becomes more widely available; and then finally a **speculative period** where numerous new enterprises are started as cheap credit is easily accessible and capital is mis-allocated again leading to a bust. Mills' view was that the psychological mood drove the availability and price of credit, i.e. the credit cycle. During the revival period, risk taking gradually increases and demand for credit increases. As lenders see profits increase and defaults decrease, they lend more and the lenders' risk taking increases. The revival period leads to speculation and then crisis, where mounting capital losses cause risk aversion among lenders and credit is restricted to the very best borrowers. Mills advocated that each period lasted approximately three years and that these three periods of three years would repeat periodically ad infinitum. John Mills is quoted as saying:

> Panics do not destroy capital; they merely reveal the extent to which it has been destroyed by its betrayal into hopelessly unproductive works.[3]

Dr. Warren F. Hickernell summarises the Mills Theory in *Financial and Business Forecasting* (1928) as follows:

> Mills bases his credit cycle theory upon two main elements; first, the tendency of human nature to exaggerate prospects for prosperity when prices rise and to underestimate business opportunities when trade is depressed. The second factor is the rate of interest, which causes wide-awake and intelligent men to expand operations when capital is abundant and to curtail operations when credit is dis-intended relative to metallic banking reserves.[4]

In addition to the nine year cycles above, American economist Joseph Kitchin discovered a shorter cycle lasting between 40 and 59 months (3 1/3 to 5 years) that was attributed to

---

[3] John Mills, article read before the Manchester Statistical Society, December 11, 1867, on Credit Cycles and the Origin of Commercial Panics. As quoted in *Financial crises and periods of industrial and commercial depression*, Burton, T. E. (1931, first published 1902).

[4] *Financial and Business Forecasting* (1928), Dr. Warren F. Hickernell.

the time lag between raw materials building up in inventories and businesses reducing output in response to falling demand.

Kuznets, Kondratieff and Schumpeter

Further cycles were identified by the American economist Simon Kuznets (a 15 to 25 year demographic/building cycle for which he won the Nobel Memorial Prize in Economic Sciences).

Russian economist Nikolai Kondratieff discovered a 45 to 60 year cycle. However the Kondratieff cycle is not accepted by modern economists due to the inability to identify a cause and also disagreement over identifying when these cycles start or finish. The cycle that Kondratieff identified appeared to cease in the post war period, which has caused many to question whether the Kondratieff cycle really exists at all, although Korotayev and Tsirel have found evidence of a 52/53 year "Kondratieff" cycle, as we shall see.

Demographic shifts in populations influence the longer cycles, as the recent boom in China has shown. A new generation of young people finishing school, finding employment, buying a car, clothes, going out with friends, buying a home, furnishing their home, having children, reaching their peak lifetime earnings, saving for retirement and living on fixed retirement incomes are predictable patterns of spending and are well known influences on business cycles.

Kitchin believed that these cycles repeated and that the larger cycles were aggregates of the smaller cycles. It is possible that these cycles are multiples of two or three nested cycles; i.e. three years, six years, nine years, 18 years, 27 years, 54 years, etc., however this is just conjecture and has not been proven.

Following the Great Depression, a huge amount of effort was put into understanding the cause of the crash and subsequent depression and also identifying the solutions that would allow the economy to recover and grow again. The long period of uncertainty that followed the 1929 crash had people believing that the roaring '20s was an aberration and that America would never achieve that level of prosperity again.

Joseph Schumpeter, who was an American economist at Harvard like Kuznets, thought differently and consolidated the then current research and thinking on these different cycles in his 1939 book *Business Cycles: A Theoretical, Historical, And Statistical Analysis of the Capitalist Process*. Schumpeter believed in a creative and destructive innovation cycle, that the Great Depression was a natural consequence of that cycle and that a new era of prosperity would come again in time. Schumpeter also believed, like Kitchin, that the different cycles were simply multiples of the shorter frequency cycles (3 x Kitchin = Juglar, 2 x Juglar = Kuznets, 3 x Kuznets = Kondratieff).

Kondratieff and spectral analysis of world GDP growth rates

Andrey Korotayev of the Russian Academy of Science and Sergey Tsirel of the University of St Petersburg sought to find evidence to support the existence of Kondratieff Waves, which they believed should be apparent in world GDP growth rates, that is if Kondratieff Waves really did exist. In 2010 they published their research paper documenting the results of their spectral analysis[5] of world GDP growth rates between 1871 and 2007. They performed two studies, one using the raw data and another in which they smoothed the actual post World War 1 and 2 annual growth rates but kept the cumulative GDP values intact. Both results showed the existence of a long wave cycle of approximately 53 years (Kondratieff) and they reported:

> ...in both spectra one can detect distinctly the Kondratieff Cycle (its period equals approximately 52-53 years)...[6]

Within the second study, using the smoothed geometric mean GDP growth rates, they noted a cycle that they identified as a Kuznets Cycle:

> As can easily be seen, within the spectra of corrected series the Kondratieff Cycle clearly dominates; however the cycle of 17-18 years is also rather salient (it can be identified as the third harmonic of the Kondratieff Cycle).[6]

Korotayev and Tsirel also stated that:

> Note that, in addition to Kuznet swings, our spectral analysis also detects a rather salient presence of economic cycles with periods 6-8 years and 3-4 years that can be tentatively identified with respectively, Juglar and Kitchin cycles.[6]

Cycle theory and study has a good pedigree, but it appears to have fallen out of fashion in recent times, at least in the mainstream media. As we can see, economists from all over the world have identified a variety of cycles attributed to different causes; credit cycles, inventory cycles, demographic cycles and commodity cycles. It seems that these different cycles are related to each other as the large cycles may be multiples of the smaller cycles. In the following chapter I'll discuss the modern view that business cycles are driven by human psychology and animal spirits before moving on to the 17.6 year stock market cycle.

---

[5] Spectral analysis is a form of data analysis that concerns a series of measurements that are ordered in time. It is used to identify cyclical patterns that may be embedded within the time series data.

[6] Korotayev, Andrey V., & Tsirel, Sergey V. 'A Spectral Analysis of World GDP Dynamics: Kondratieff Waves, Kuznets Swings, Juglar and Kitchin Cycles in Global Economic Development, and the 2008–2009 Economic Crisis'. *Structure and Dynamics*. 2010. Vol.4. #1. P.3-57.

CHAPTER 3

Business Cycles –
A Modern Psychological Perspective

You make most of your money in a bear market, you just don't realize it at the time.

The above quote from Shelby Cullom Davis is worth remembering, as bear markets inevitably lead to investors losing faith with the stock market. As stock market prices stagnate, however, quality stocks become better value as gradually improving company earnings, arising from a steady improvement in trade and employment, are not fully reflected in equity prices. For long-term investors, providing that they have cash to put to work, the ability to buy good quality stocks cheaply ahead of a new bull market is a twice in a lifetime opportunity.

The lower the price initially paid, the more will be made in the end – the old mantra of buy low, sell high. However, during a market correction or general sideways action it often doesn't feel like progress is being made which is why so many investors abandon equities during bear markets.

It is therefore important to recognise the regular bull and bear phases that occur in the stock market and adapt our investment approach, along with our expectations, to fit the stock market conditions.

Characteristics of bull and bear markets

The term *bull market* is used to describe a market where the overriding trend is up. Bull markets are characterised by increasing investor optimism that stock prices will continue to rise because of increasing company profits. The rising enthusiasm for stocks often leads investors to pay higher prices in anticipation of higher future profits. The increased participation in stocks by investors during a bull market often pushes valuations to unsustainably high levels.

In contrast, a *bear market* is a market where the overriding trend is down. Bear markets are characterised by investor pessimism that stock prices will continue to fall or that prices will not rise because of falling or stagnating company profits. The increased distrust of stocks often leads to investors projecting the current difficult conditions into the future and they are unwilling to pay too much for uncertain future profits. Investors often abandon the stock market in search of better performing markets such as bonds and commodities and prices fall to very low valuations, reflecting the lower interest in stocks.

The changes in investor optimism and pessimism, that I have described above, fits well with our discussion in the previous chapter regarding John Mills and the changing psychological mood of the masses. Psychology has a huge part to play in the stock markets, as well as business cycles. Every day millions of stock market participants are making individual buy and sell decisions. Every once in a while popular opinion converges on an idea that is so compelling that the investment community and general public collectively lose their minds and a mania takes hold. The "New Economy" was a classic example of this and although the internet revolution did change the world, profits still rule how companies are valued and positive cash-flow is a definite requirement.

We shall see in Chapter 4 that stock market manias, the boom and busts that occur from time to time as part of the speculative period, happen at the end of the 18 year bull market cycle and lead to the 18 year bear market that follows.

Dr . Warren F. Hickernell referred to booms and busts as follows:

> Intelligent men furnish the initial impulse toward expansion when business is depressed, and they are followed by the ignorant. Later, the intelligent contract operations when inflation appears, but the ignorant expand excessively until checked by a crisis. In a state of panic, the ignorant curtail abnormally.[7]

There appears to be something inherent within human biology that encourages people to extrapolate past performance into the future, without noticing when the underlying conditions have changed.

Human biology

Dr John Coates, former Wall Street trader turned neuroscientist, and author of *The Hour Between Dog and Wolf*, explained in a *Time* magazine article how his research into psychology and neuroscience indicates that a stock market trader's winning streak can change the trader's biology in such a way that it may eventually lead to excessive risk taking and over-confidence.

---

[7] *Financial and Business Forecasting* (1928), Dr. Warren F. Hickernell.

Coates and his colleagues at the University of Cambridge conducted experiments on a trading floor and identified that:

> …under circumstances of extraordinary opportunity otherwise known as a winning streak our biology can overreact, and our risk taking become pathological. [8]

The 'winner effect', a model from animal behaviour, illustrates how this can occur:

> When males enter a fight or competition their testosterone surges which increases their hemoglobin and hence their blood's capacity to carry oxygen; and in the brain it increases confidence and appetite for risk. The winner emerges with even higher levels of testosterone and this heightens his chances of winning yet again, leading to a positive feedback loop.

> Effective risk-taking morphs into over-confidence and dangerous behaviour and traders on a winning streak may take on positions of ever-increasing size, with ever worsening risk-reward trade-offs.[8]

The opposite is true during a crisis:

> The uncertainty people feel during a crisis can raise stress hormone to such an extent that they promote feelings of anxiety, a selective recall of disturbing memories, and a tendency to find danger where none exists. Among traders and investors the stress response may foster an irrational risk-aversion, impairing their ability to manage positions put on in more optimistic times.[8]

Human biology therefore engenders a positive feedback loop when we are winning and a tendency to become over confident and think that our success is down to our infallible skill – this leads to the taking of greater and greater risks. Conversely, when the inevitable bust occurs an equivalent negative feedback loop occurs and irrational risk aversion takes hold. Coates was describing the behaviour of an individual but if his logic is applied to a group of people, such as stock market participants, it can be seen how a long successful period can lead to excessive risk taking that in turn leads to major booms and subsequent busts.

Two recent events sprang to mind when reading Coates' article. The first one involves Gordon Brown, the UK Chancellor of the Exchequer from 1997 to 2007. In his 1997 Labour government pre-budget report he said:

> For 40 years our economy has an unenviable history, under governments of both parties, of boom and bust.

---

[8] http://ideas.time.com/2012/06/21/the-anatomy-of-a-huge-trading-loss

So, against a background of mounting uncertainty and instability in the global economy, we set about establishing a new economic framework to secure long-term economic stability and put an end to the damaging cycle of boom and bust.

And in his last budget as Chancellor in 2007 he said:

we will never return to the old boom and bust.[9]

Here is a man who clearly believed his own rhetoric that he had abolished boom and bust; as a result the UK was running a large budget deficit during one of the largest economic booms in history. Clearly someone with a better grasp of economic history would have realised the risk they were taking. "The ignorant expand excessively until checked by a crisis," as Dr. Warren F. Hickernell said.

The second recent event concerns Citigroup's ex-CEO Chuck Prince and is one of my favourite quotes of all time. Talking to the *Financial Times* about the growing credit crunch in July 2007 and the risks Citigroup faced Prince said:

When the music stops, in terms of liquidity, things will be complicated. But as long as the music is playing, you've got to get up and dance. We're still dancing.[10]

A few short months later Prince resigned after Citigroup's Q3 results showed a surge in late payments on consumer mortgages. The music had probably already stopped when Prince made his statement.

George Soros – Reflexivity

John Coates' work is also aligned with George Soros' theory of reflexivity as described in his book *The Alchemy of Finance*. Soros argues that stock market prices are determined by two factors:

1. The underlying trend of the market.

2. The expectations of market participants (prevailing bias).

So far so uncontroversial – underlying market conditions provide the overall trend and profit expectations generally dictate a company's share price. Soros' argument gets interesting however because he suggests that the company's share price can influence the company's fundamental prospects and therefore that the level of the stock market can influence the expectations of the market participants.

---

[9] http://www.channel4.com/news/articles/politics/domestic_politics/factcheck+no+more+boom+and+bust/2564157.html

[10] http://business.time.com/2007/07/10/citigroups_chuck_prince_wants

This assertion of Soros' seems completely reasonable. How many times do people extrapolate past performance into the future when trying to look for a place to invest their capital? Regardless of the standard warning that the value of your investment can go down as well as up, commercial property funds were an easy sell in 2007 due to their recent outperformance and the newspapers were full of adverts for them. Similarly, China funds were also an easy sell in 2007. While the music plays (investors are gullible enough to invest with them), they dance.

Whether it is called reflexivity, animal spirits or irrational exuberance, these terms are describing the same thing and the outcome is that markets reach a point where they take on a life of their own. The markets feed on their own inflated expectations to such a degree that eventually the expectations that are priced into the market cannot be satisfied. Once this occurs a panic develops and a rapid crisis occurs.

FIGURE 1 - PROFILE OF REFLEXIVE MARKETS

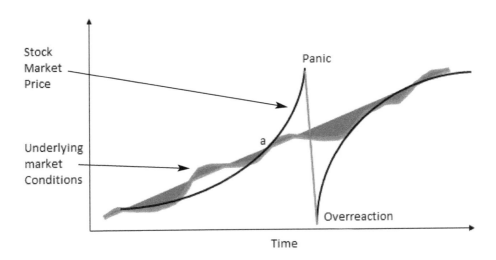

Figure 1 shows reflexivity in action. The stock market trend is up as underlying market conditions turn favourable and sentiment changes as market participants anticipate the economy coming out of recession. At point 'a' the market has caught up with reality and markets represent fair value (market prices match unbiased rational expectations). The stock market price rise continues, however, and market participants are now anticipating ever increasing amounts for future profits on the basis that this trend will continue indefinitely (possibly based on a technological revolution such as the internet). At this point the market starts to rise exponentially and becomes detached from the underlying market conditions that have changed. When reality reasserts itself due to an unexpected event, the emperor is seen to have no clothes and a crash occurs.

Juglar and Mills have described the business cycle as consisting of prosperity (revival period), leading to a speculative period, followed by a post panic period. Soros has described the boom and bust process based on expectations and an underlying trend. Coates has described the mechanism for expectations (risk taking) increasing based on previous success, to the point that they are too far removed from the underlying trend and where disappointment is the only outcome that remains.

We can see that bubbles and panics occur predominately due to human nature and this has been the case throughout history:

- During tulip mania in Holland in 1637, rare, colourful tulip bulbs were being traded at ever fanciful prices. At the top of the bubble some bulbs were changing hands for the value of a house.

- The South Sea bubble in 1720 arose from the South Sea Company buying the rights to all trade in the South Seas (South America). Speculative demand for the company, which was yet to make a profit, soared as investors anticipated large future profits from this monopoly. At the top of the bubble shares were priced at £1,000 each having been £100 one year before.

- The 1929 stock market bubble was initially driven by economic prosperity but was soon driven by a speculative bubble where ordinary people thought they couldn't lose by investing in shares. The market fell 89% and took 25 years to recover its previous high.

More recently there was the 2000 dotcom bubble and the 2007 housing bubble where investors once again underestimated the risks and overestimated the rewards. There are psychological and neurological characteristics that lead investors to take more risk and become increasingly confident until they are stopped by a crisis. These human characteristics lead to patterns of behaviour that recur over time and there is no reason to believe that the future will be any different. However, Coates and Soros do not mention any timescales in which this will occur.

The following chapter introduces the Balenthiran 17.6 Year Stock Market Cycle and demonstrates its validity through five distinct cycles: the bear market from 1929 to 1947, the bull market from 1947 to 1965, the bear market from 1965 to 1982, the bull market from 1982 to 2000 and the current bear market from 2000 to today, including the intermediate turning points and when I expect this current bear market to end. We shall see that important turning points associated with stock market crashes and trend changes occur at specific points within the Balenthiran Cycle, with a defined periodicity, and the major boom and bust occurs at the end of the Balenthiran Cycle. This provides the knowledgeable with the opportunity to profit as it can be precisely identified which cycle the market is in and where it is in the cycle.

CHAPTER 4

Balenthiran 17.6 Year
Stock Market Cycle

Many investors agree that no one ever really knows which way the market will move. Nothing could be further from the truth. We discovered that while stocks do indeed fluctuate, they do so in well-defined, often predictable patterns. These patterns recur too frequently to be a result of chance or coincidence.

Jeffery Hirsch and Yale Hirsch, *The Stock Trader's Almanac*

At this point it is briefly worth recapping what has been covered so far:

- In chapter 1 we saw that studies have confirmed the existence of regular cycles in commodities and stocks that average 18 years in duration, and these cycles alternate between commodities and stocks in terms of outperformance.

- In chapter 2 we saw that regular business cycles have been identified by leading 20th century economists and that cycles of approximately three, six, nine, 18 and 54 years feature prominently.

- In chapter 3 we saw that there are psychological and neurological aspects of human biology that lead to greater levels of risk taking and ultimately self-reinforcing cycles of boom and bust.

I have also touched on some of the possible causes of the documented business cycles; supply and demand, over/under investment, credit availability and pricing. What we have seen is that business cycles are widely recognised and that human psychology, in the form of increasing expectations, plays some part in this. As we can't change human nature, it is likely that the behaviour patterns of the past will continue into the future.

It is my belief that if cycles exist, and as we have seen modern economists are agreed that they do, then these cycles should be identifiable in the stock market, as the stock market represents the market capitalization of the biggest businesses, covering all areas of the economy, as well as the decisions of millions of investors.

Figure 2 shows nominal US GDP per capita and the Dow Jones Industrial Index from 1897 to 2011, rebased to 100 and in logarithmic scale. Rising GDP per capita indicates growth in the economy, possibly from a rise in productivity, and this growth should lead to a rise in corporate profits and therefore the stock market. Although the two lines diverge from time to time, it can be seen that GDP per capita growth and stock market appreciation trend up over the long term with GDP per capita leading the stock market.

FIGURE 2 - US GDP PER CAPITA VS. DOW JONES INDUSTRIAL INDEX (REBASED TO 100)

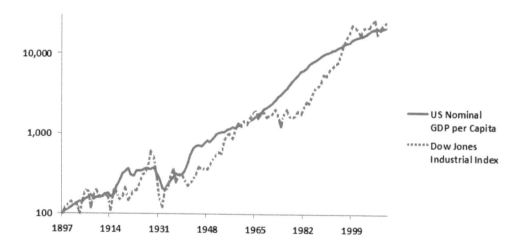

Source data: MeasuringWorth.com and research.stlouisfed.org

The premise behind the Balenthiran Cycle is that waves of optimism and pessimism have a cyclical rhythm which can be used to predict market sentiment. This is not to say that the cycle can necessarily predict the dates of stock market highs and lows with any degree of precision, however in practice it has identified a number of key reversal points, as I shall demonstrate. In addition, different phases of the cycle have different characteristics that are broadly similar from cycle to cycle.

Stock market cycles

As explained in the Introduction, cycles are a sequence of events that repeat over time and a number of cycles have been documented in relation to the stock market. A good example of a stock market cycle is the US presidential cycle where it has been demonstrated that political influences typically lead to an increased stock market performance in years three and four of a president's four year term.

Two other commonly referred to stock market cycles are *cyclical cycles* and *secular cycles*. Cyclical cycles are shorter term cycles of about four years that comprise bull and bear market phases lasting a couple of years. Secular cycles are longer term cycles of about 30 to 40 years that comprise secular bull and secular bear markets of about half this time. The bull market from 1982 to 2000 was a secular bull market, and since 2000 stocks have been in a secular bear market, however there was a cyclical bull market between 2003 and 2007 and again from 2009 to 2011.

The Balenthiran Cycle

As mentioned in the introduction, I have identified a 17.6 year cycle that exists in the stock market and I have called this cycle the Balenthiran Cycle. The Balenthiran Cycle consists of increments of 2.2 years, together with specific intermediate (cyclical) turning points that repeat within the 17.6 year cycle. There is a different sequence for secular bull markets and secular bear markets and together these form a Secular cycle of length 35.2 years.

Profile of a bull market

The Balenthiran Cycle follows the pattern shown in Figure 3.

FIGURE 3 - PROFILE OF A BULL MARKET

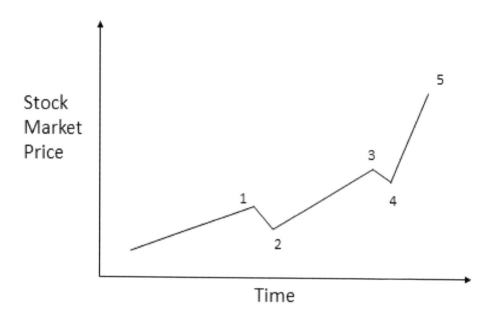

- Phase 1 – an uptrend lasting 4 to 5 years
- Phase 2 – a short sharp correction with no overall progress for 1 to 2 years
- Phase 3 – a strong market rally lasting 4 to 5 years
- Phase 4 – a mild mid cycle correction
- Phase 5 – major 18 year bull market top (mania phase)

In order to determine the cycle dates the bullish phases are said to be 4.4 years in duration and the bearish phases are 2.2 years in duration (see the appendix for more information on how I discovered the 2.2 and 4.4 year cycles). It is important to note that during the bearish phases, the exact low point may be towards the beginning of that 2.2 year period, but the general negative mood will persist during the whole period.

The bull market can be shown as follows:

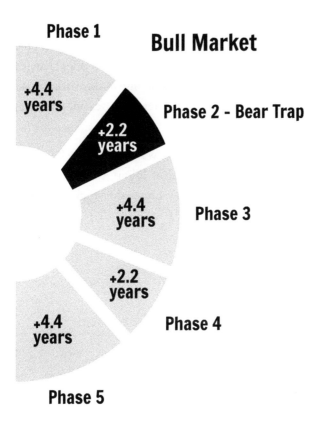

Phase 2 is often described as a bear trap where investors tend to believe that the run up in the market was a bear market rally and that further falls are likely so they start selling or shorting. They do not believe the uptrend was a new bull market until later in the bull market and are forced to buy back in at higher prices, further fuelling the bull-run. Phase 4 in a bull market is often a period of volatility but ultimately it is a period to continue to be long until the final blow off top occurs.

Elliott Waves

Some readers may think that Figure 3 looks like an Elliott Wave, but what is described here is not an Elliott Wave as such.

Elliott Waves are specific recurring chart patterns based on changes in investor psychology and were discovered by Ralph Nelson Elliott. Elliott's chart patterns arise from changes in fear and greed and the natural human reaction that occurs in response to the market making a new high (greed/fear of missing out on more gains) or a new low (fear of even bigger losses).

The key difference between the Balenthiran Cycle and Elliott Waves is that the Balenthiran Cycle has distinct phases of fixed time and direction, whereas Elliott Waves do not. Also the Balenthiran Cycle is not trying to determine by how much the stock market may increase or decrease in that time.

Profile of a bear market

In a bear market the Balenthiran Cycle follows the pattern shown in Figure 4.

FIGURE 4 - PROFILE OF A BEAR MARKET

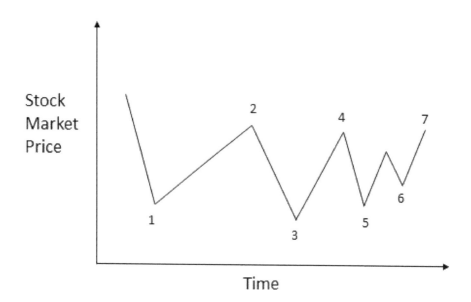

- Phase 1 – an initial bear market crash lasting approximately 2 years

- Phase 2 – a bear market rally lasting 4 to 5 years

- Phase 3 – a second bear market crash lasting approximately 2 years (often the lowest low)

- Phase 4 – a second bear market rally lasting approximately 2 years

- Phase 5 – major 18 year bear market low (not necessarily the lowest low)

- Phase 6 – a final bear market low

- Phase 7 – end of 18 year bear market

Once again in order to determine the cycle dates the bullish phases are said to be 4.4 years in duration and the bearish phases are 2.2 years in duration. It is important to note that in some cases during the bearish phases, the exact low point may be towards the beginning of that 2.2 year period, but the general negative mood will persist during the whole period.

The bear market can be shown as follows:

The phase 3 bear market often marks the lowest lows of the whole bear market. As we shall see, the crash during the phase 5 high often marks the low prior to the new bull market, and can often be a good place to buy equities at bargain prices prior to the new bull market starting after phase 6. Phases 6 and 7 are often characterised by choppy markets and prices can drift higher and lower.

We will now study key stock market periods from the past 100 years to demonstrate the Balenthiran Cycle in action.

PART I: BULL MARKET 1982 TO 2000

To compare the performance of the actual market with the Balenthiran Cycle, a bull market shall be taken first. Bull markets are simpler in form and as there has only recently been the passing of the last great bull market from 1982 to 2000, the bull market is reasonably fresh in memory and the key dates will be familiar to most of us.

The 1980s and 1990s bull market was a wonder to behold and it certainly lifted the prosperity of masses. Whether you were an investor or not these were feel good times. The 1987 crash was a time that I remember very well. I was still a child and there had been a great storm that had closed my school. The storm disrupted many trains into London, meaning traders were struggling to get into the City. Panic took hold in a major way, starting in the US. Over the next few days this panic travelled around the world and the Dow Jones Industrial Average (DJIA) fell by 36%. As Figure 5 shows it took two years to exceed the 1987 high and for the bull market to confirm its upward trend.

FIGURE 5: DJIA (1980 TO 2000 DAILY)

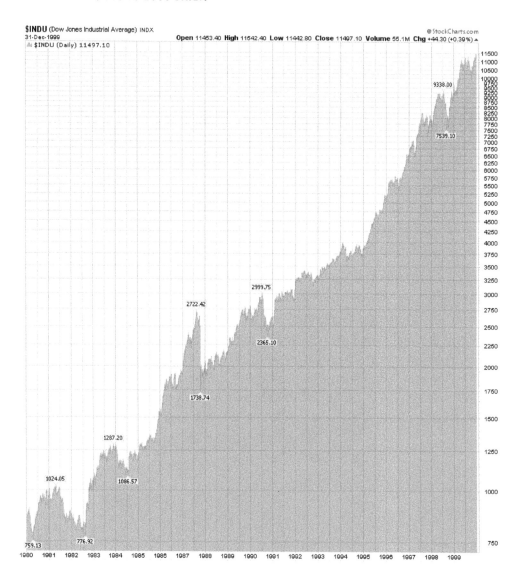

Source: Stockcharts.com

Looking at Figure 5 you may be questioning whether the bull market actually started in 1980 rather than 1982 as that was a lower low. 1980 looks like a reasonable place for the bull market to begin, however the bull market undoubtedly ended in 2000 and taking the 18 year cycle into consideration I took 1982 as the starting point for the bull market. As we shall see, 1982 fits the cycle when extrapolated back to 1929, and 1982 was also identified as the start of the bull market by stock market historian Russell Napier in his book *Anatomy of the Bear*.

By visually inspecting the chart we can see that the key highs and lows were:

	Year	Value	Approximate Interval
Bear Market Low	1982	776.92	
High	1987	2722.42	5 years
Low	1987	1738.74	2 months
Bull Market High	2000	11772.98	13 years

By taking the key dates of 1982, 1987 and 2000, I initially developed the idealised cycle model that would also fit the previous 100 years of market activity. The initial starting point was that the bull market rallies lasted approximately five years and the crashes lasted approximately two years until the uptrend resumed. This two year crash period also worked with the dotcom bust from 2000 to 2002 and the credit crunch from 2007 to 2009. A five year uptrend also followed from 2002 to the property induced stock market top of 2007.

FIGURE 6: DJIA (1980 TO 2000 DAILY) UPTREND

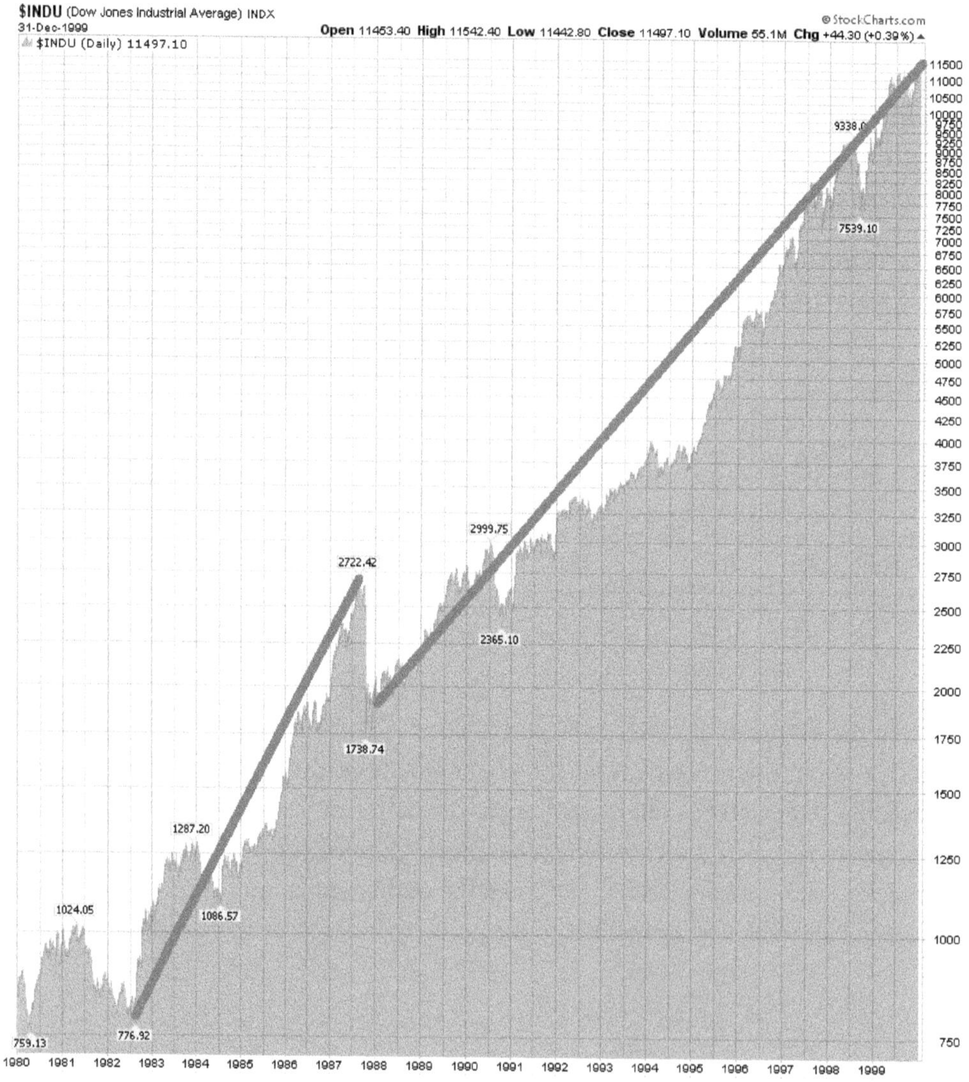

Source: Stockcharts.com

Idealised bull stock market cycle

Having identified the key points of 1982, 1987 and 2000, and because I wanted the uptrend to be a multiple of the downtrend, the five year uptrends and two year downtrends were gradually refined. The first stage was to link these dates in such a way that they would also coincide with other key dates, such as 2007, 2009 and also 1929. As I discuss in the appendix, it wasn't a straightforward logical process that brought me to this point. There were numerous false starts and through a process of trial and error I discovered the 2.2 year and 4.4 year cycles. Eventually the idealised bull stock market cycle was constructed as follows:

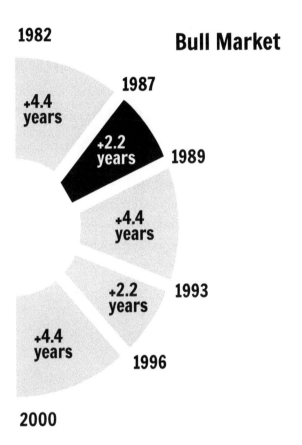

Figure 6 shows that there were two key uptrends during which it was important to be fully invested during the 1980s/90s bull market. With the benefit of hindsight we can see that it was actually best to be fully invested during this whole period.

The DJIA nearly tripled by the first high point in 1987. By the end of 1989 the DJIA was hovering near the previous high of 2720 and the bull market continued. Buying in late 1987 and holding until 2000 would have yielded a spectacular near six-fold gain! Figure 6 shows a broadly flat picture between 1994 and 1995 and then a rapid increase in 1996, so the best strategy would have been to continue to hold during this period.

There were big corrections in 1990 and 1998 but these were followed by quick recoveries and within 12 months the bull market was making new highs. These corrections have therefore been ignored. 1993 and 1996 are shown for completeness due to this being a cyclical model.

In summary, we can see that the two key periods in the 1982 to 2000 bull market were 1982 to 1987 and 1989 to 2000, and that the model correctly identified all four years. This may seem easy for this short period, however we shall see that this model works for the 1947 to 1965 stock market bull as well.

Before we look at another bull market we shall look at the other half of the model.

We have seen how the bull market unfolded and we know what happened next, but when will this financial crisis end? In order to think about bear markets it is insightful to revisit the great bear market following the crash of 1929. The period after 1929 is similar to the current situation – large amounts of debt in the global economy that countries are finding it difficult to service and interest rates at record lows with little growth – so we can learn a lot from this period. We will come back to the post 2000 period and to what is in store for the future at the end of this chapter.

PART II: BEAR MARKET 1929 TO 1947

Prior to the 2000 dotcom bubble bursting, the crash that most people referred to was the 1929 stock market crash and the Great Depression that followed. The DJIA peaked on 3 September 1929 at 381.17 and subsequently fell to 41.22, an incredible decline of 89%. This is a great place to start our quest to understand the cyclical characteristics of bear markets.

FIGURE 7: DJIA (1920 TO 1940 DAILY)

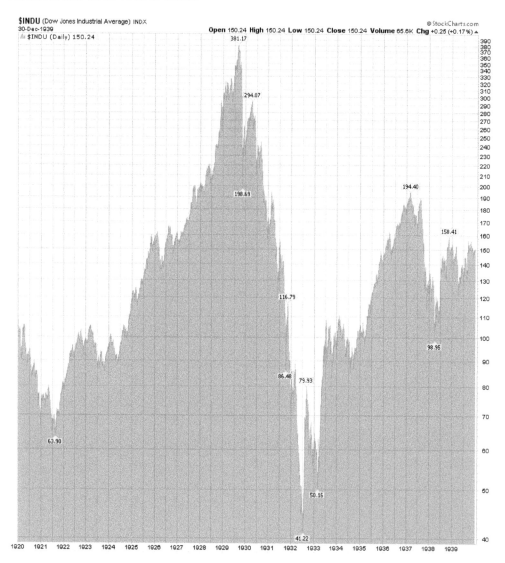

Source: Stockcharts.com

Figure 7 shows the strength of the initial crash over a period of two to three years. However this wasn't the end of the bear market. The market more than quadrupled between 1932 to 1937 and then fell by nearly a half again by 1942 (Figure 8). These huge swings are not the characteristics of a bull market; instead they are the actions of a secular bear market. Figure 8 shows that the 1929 highs were not exceeded until 1954 – some 25 years later!

FIGURE 8: DJIA (1940 TO 1960 DAILY)

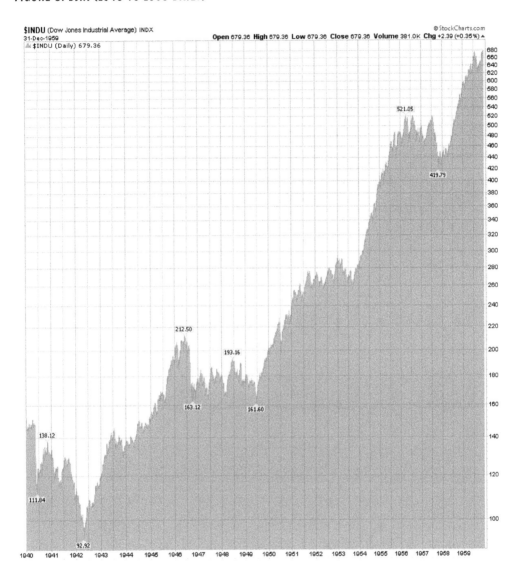

Source: Stockcharts.com

So when was the best time to buy and when did the bear market end?

On first inspection 1942 looks like the end of the bear market and therefore a great time to buy – it was the bottom after all. But 1946 saw a 23% stock market crash and nearly five years of sideways price movements, so 1942 wasn't the end of the bear market. Somewhere between 1946 and 1950 appears to be when the bear market ended and that puts us in the range of a bear market lasting 17 to 21 years before a sustained uptrend began.

By visually inspecting Figure 9 and Figure 10 we can see that the key highs and lows were:

	Year	Value	Approximate Interval
Bull Market High	1929	381.17	
Bear Market Low	1932	41.22	3 years
High	1937	194.40	5 years
Low	1938	98.95	1 year
High	1938	158.41	6 months
Low	1942	92.62	4 years
High	1946	212.50	4 years
Low	1946	163.12	6 months

FIGURE 9: DJIA (1920 TO 1940 DAILY) DOWNTREND

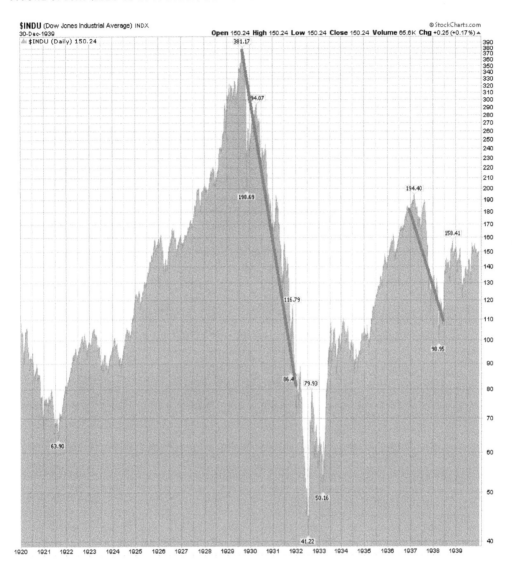

Source: Stockcharts.com

FIGURE 10: DJIA (1940 TO 1960 DAILY) DOWNTREND

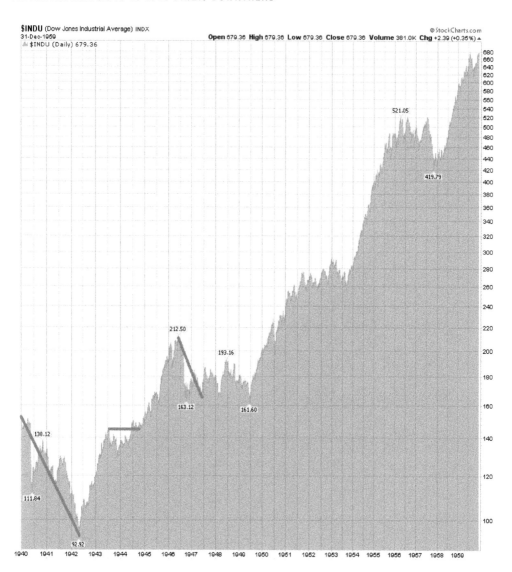

Source: Stockcharts.com

Idealised bear stock market cycle

Using uptrends of 4.4 years and downtrends of 2.2 years the idealised bear stock market cycle is as follows:

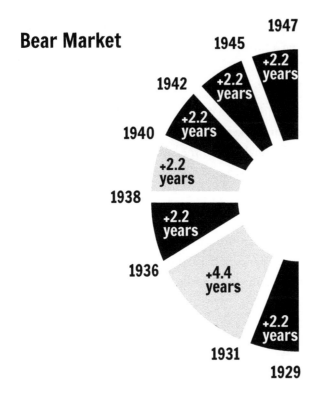

How does the idealised cycle model match up against the real stock market?

	Year	Value	Comments
Bull Market High	1929	381.27	Correct
Low	1931	86.48	The low was actually in 1932 at 41.22
High	1936	184.90	The high was actually in 1937 at 194.40
Low	1938	98.95	Correct
High	1940	152.80	The high was in 1938 at 158.41
Low	1942	92.92	Correct
End of Bear Market	1947	163.21	Correct

During the bear market from 1929 to 1947 there were three market drops (1929 to 1932, 1937 to 1938 and 1939 to 1942) and three subsequent bear market rallies.

The model correctly identified the three bear periods and the final low shortly after phase 5 (1942). The highs in 1936 and 1940 were within 5% of the actual market highs.

However one notable exception was that there were significant falls after 1931 and the market didn't bottom until it had fallen a further 50% in 1932.

Conclusion

The key points to note are the correct identification of the start and end of the bear market and a fairly good roadmap for future bear market rallies and sell offs. Also note that there was a nasty sell off in 1942 that marked a final low for the bear market. Although the new bull market did not begin until 1947, 1942 was an excellent year to start investing for the next bull market.

In the next section the idealised bull market model that was demonstrated for the period 1982 to 2000 will be applied to the bull market from 1947 to 1965, and the idealised bear market model that has just been seen for the period 1929 to 1947 will be applied to the bear market from 1965 to 1982. It will be shown that the idealised models fit these later periods perfectly.

PART III: BULL MARKET 1947 TO 1965 AND BEAR MARKET 1965 TO 1982

Now that a bull market and a bear market have been analysed and compared to the Balenthiran Cycle, let's see how a full cycle from bear to bull and back to bear compares. The period from 1947 to 1965 and then to 1982 fits this criteria.

Balenthiran Cycle Model

Putting together the bull and bear sections of the idealised stock market cycle, the following cycle is produced:

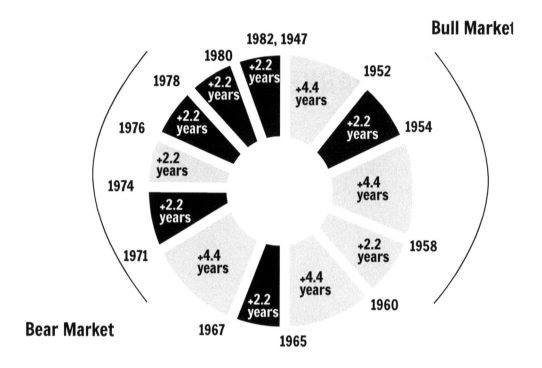

If the cycle that fits the 1980/90s and 1930/40s is correct then it should be easy to identify the same cyclical pattern during the bull market from 1947 to 1965 and the bear market from 1965 to 1982.

1947 to 1965 bull market

It is easy to identify bull markets in hindsight; you can see in Figure 11 and Figure 12 that from 1947 the DJIA was in a clear bull market until the mid 1960s. Equally the 1970s bear market was a period of sideways stock market movements.

FIGURE 11: DJIA (1940 TO 1960 DAILY)

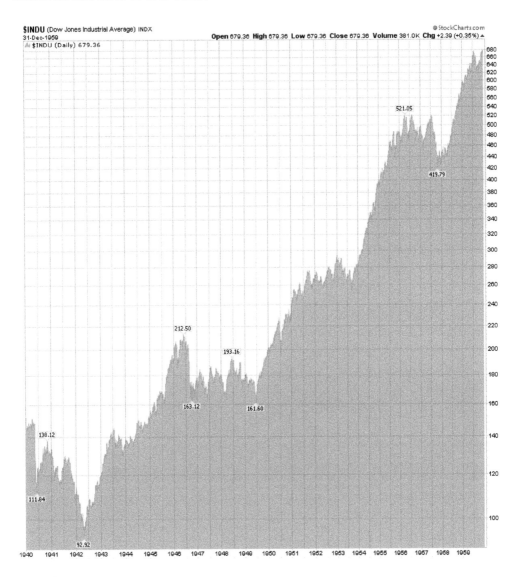

Source: Stockcharts.com

FIGURE 12: DJIA (1960 TO 1980 DAILY)

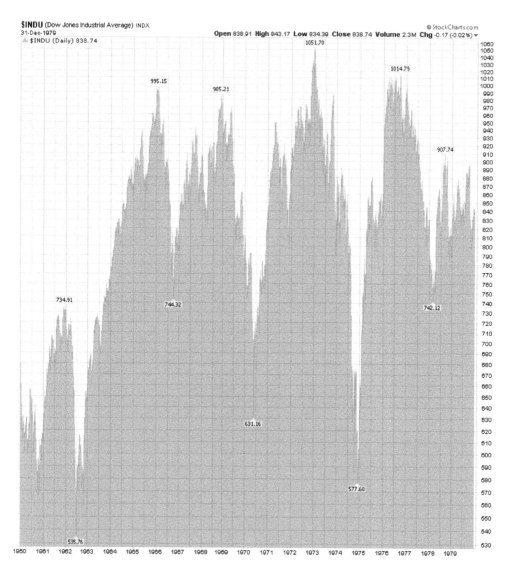

Source: Stockcharts.com

How does the Balenthiran Cycle Model match up against the real stock market?

	Year	Value	Comments
Bull Market Start	1947	163.21	Correct
High	1952	29200	Correct
Start of Phase 3	1954	279.87	The low was in 1953 at 255.49
Bull Market High	1965	969.26	The high was actually in 1966 at 995.15

FIGURE 13: DJIA (1940 TO 1960 DAILY) UPTREND

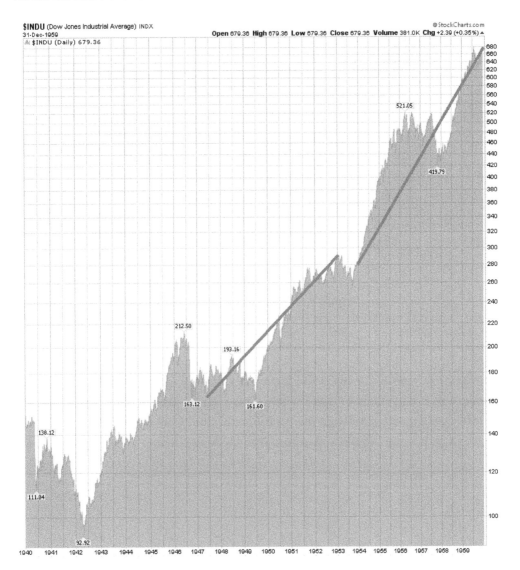

The Balenthiran Cycle Model's accuracy during the 1947 to 1965 bull market is very good (see Figure 13). The highs and lows are within 5% to 10% of the actual market tops or bottoms even though the year may have been slightly early or late. The beginning of the final bull market (phases 3, 4 & 5) starts in 1954 when the stock market surpassed its 1952 high. The model provides the confidence to buy and hold over an 18 year period.

1965 to 1982 bear market

Looking at the bear market from 1965 to 1982 (see Figure 14) we see the same cyclical pattern that we saw in the 1930s.

	Year	Value	Comments
Bull Market High	1965	969.26	The high was actually in 1966 at 995.15
Low	1967	786.41	The low was actually in 1966 at 744.32
High	1971	950.82	The high was actually in 1972 at 1051.70
Low	1974	577.60	Correct
High	1976	1014.9	Correct
Phase 4 Low	1978	742.12	Correct
Low	1980	759.13	Correct
End of Bear Market	1982	776.92	Correct

Once again the years of the highs and lows as per the Balenthiran Cycle Model are very accurate and within 5% to 10% of the actual market tops and bottoms. The model has provided a good roadmap for stock market behaviour from 1947 to 1982. All that remains is to see what the model thinks will happen from 2000 to 2018.

FIGURE 14: DJIA (1960 TO 1980 DAILY) DOWNTREND

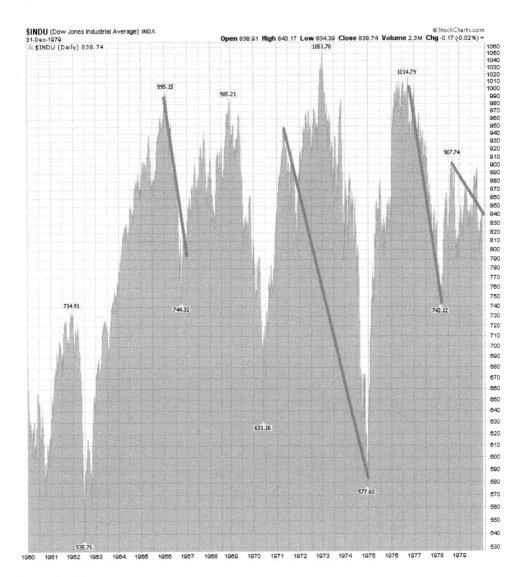

Source: Stockcharts.com

PART IV: BEAR MARKET 2000 TO 2018

This is the most interesting part and the answer to the questions posed in the introduction; was the 2009 stock market low the end of the bear market? When does the current bear market end and the new bull market begin?

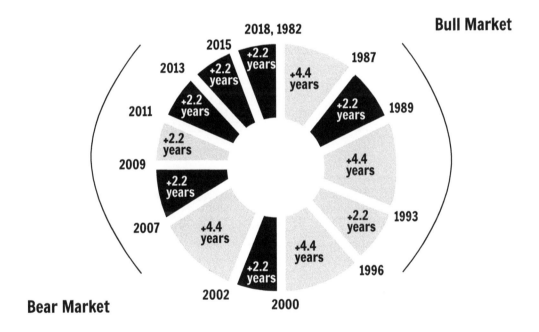

FIGURE 15: DJIA (2000 TO 2012 DAILY)

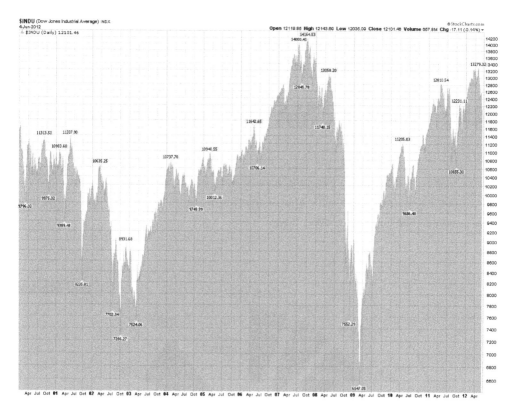

Source: Stockcharts.com

Again, the Balenthiran Cycle Model shall be compared against the actual stock market.

It is immediately obvious from Figure 15 that there is a good match and in fact on closer inspection (see Figure 16) there is actually a perfect match for the initial part of the bear market that has occurred so far.

	Year	Value	Comments
Bear Market Start	2000	11772.98	Correct
Low	2002	7286.27	Correct
High	2007	14164.53	Correct
Bear Market Low	2009	6547.05	Correct
High	2011	12810.54	Correct
Phase 4 Low	2013	?	Final low. Not likely to be lower than that seen in 2009, but ideally below the 2011 high. A good entry point for new bull market?
Low	2015	?	?
End of Bear Market	2018	?	Start of the new bull market?

FIGURE 16: DJIA (2000 TO 2012 DAILY) DOWNTREND

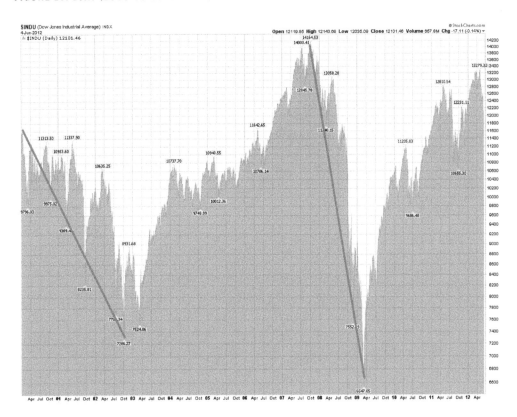

Source: Stockcharts.com

The model has correctly identified 2000, 2002, 2007 and 2009 as pivotal points in the current bear market. At the time of writing I don't know whether there will be a significant low in 2013, but there is every reason to think that during 2013 there will be a final significant low for this bear market.

We have seen how accurately the Balenthiran Cycle identifies the start and end of secular bull and bear markets together with the cyclical counter trend rallies or crashes. The Balenthiran Cycle does not predict market tops or bottoms but rather it forecasts shifts in investor sentiment which will lead to the market changing direction. As we shall see in the following chapter, this information allows the patient investor to choose a strategy to be on the right side of the bull/bear market and to plan an investment approach years in advance.

CHAPTER 5

How To Trade The Balenthiran 17.6
Year Stock Market Cycle

Exactly where we are in the larger cycle is difficult to determine. I must confess I have been confused on the issue since 1982.

George Soros, *The Alchemy of Finance*

Exactly where we are in any given stock market cycle is a constant source of confusion among investors. Now that we have seen that the Balenthiran Cycle accurately identifies the start and end of secular bull and bear markets, together with intermediate turning points, this information can be used to plan for the future. It can forecast with a high degree of confidence that market lows are expected in 2013, 2015 and 2018, and that 2013 should be the last significant market low of this bear market. Although there will be continued volatility after 2013, there should see higher lows after 2013; 2013 therefore represents a good time to start accumulating equities for the next bull market starting in 2018.

Different stock market conditions call for different investment strategies. Buy and hold has been a disaster for millions of investors since 2000 and yet this same strategy worked brilliantly throughout the 1980s and 1990s. We have seen how the stock market changes its character and the Balenthiran Cycle should be used to anticipate when the investment landscape is likely to change.

An important point to note is that the Balenthiran Cycle identifies changes in market sentiment. It should not be used for picking exact market tops and bottoms but rather looking for when to change investment approach to suit the changing markets. With that in mind it is the investor's individual investment strategy that will dictate their trading approach and how they use the cycle.

Complete Balenthiran Cycle Model

The complete Balenthiran Cycle Model looks like this:

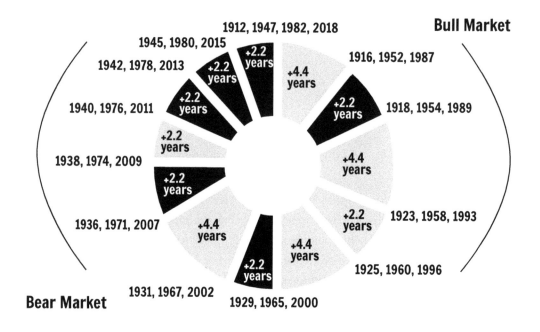

As can be seen from Figure 17, the model correctly identifies the 17.6 year periods in which there were bull markets or bear markets over more than 100 years, and we have seen that it also identifies the intermediate turning points.

FIGURE 17: DJIA (1900 TO 2012 DAILY)

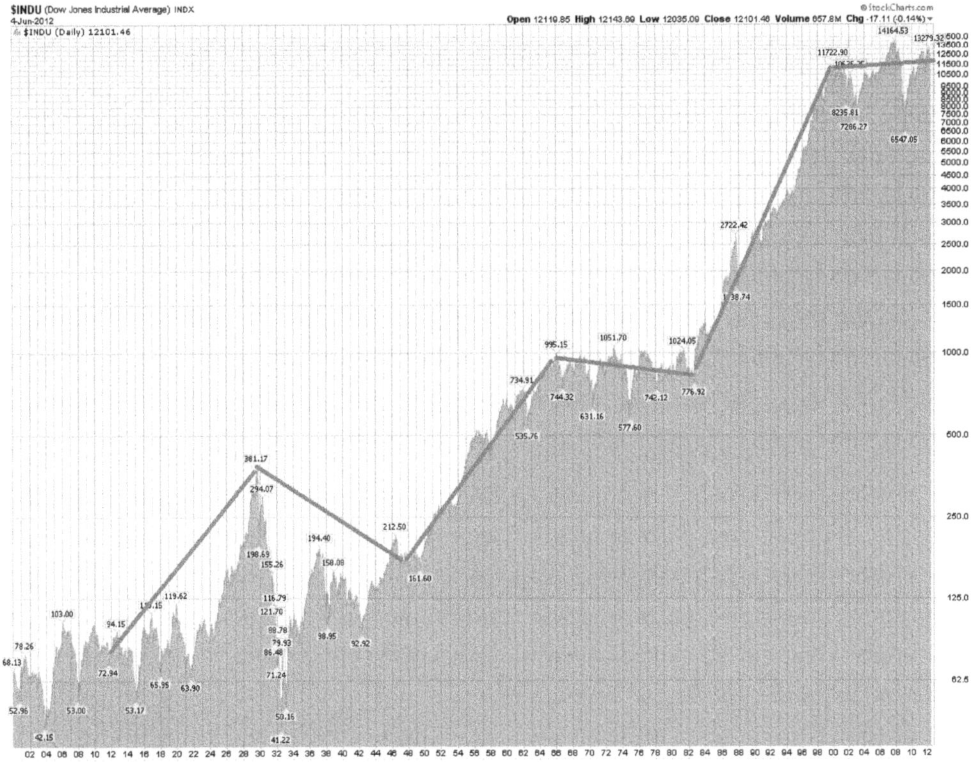

Source: Stockcharts.com

The cycle is like a roadmap; it tells you how to get somewhere but you still have to do the driving. Traffic, accidents, weather and also the driver impact the journey. The destination is the same but each driver will have a different journey. Similarly the cycle can guide an investor but each investor still needs to utilise their own investment skills to determine what to buy and precisely when.

I am now going to consider what investment strategies to deploy during the coming years and how to trade the Balenthiran Cycle.

Transition from bullish to bearish periods

A long only investor will want to consider moving from being fully invested in the equity markets to partially invested and holding increasing amounts of cash to reinvest during the sell offs. A long and short investor will want to consider closing some long positions and moving from being net long to net short overall.

All investors need to consider their overall asset allocations and start to reduce their equity exposure and increase their exposure to other asset classes (cash, commodities, bonds, etc.). It is best to scale out of positions leading up to the year of the trend change in order to take profits while keeping some exposure to further gains.

A trading approach is required during bear markets, i.e. buy on dips, hedge or sell on rallies. I personally find that a value-orientated investing approach works well, focusing on fundamentals such as cash-flow, dividend yield, dividend cover, earning per share growth and net debt. Other metrics such as discount to net asset value, high cash balances and acquisitive management can also be used. During a recession the weakest leave the market place and the strongest will remain to take full advantage of the new period of economic expansion. These are the companies I want to be invested in. The bear market is expected to last 18 years but some companies will do very well during this period, therefore it would be wrong to be completely out of the equity markets for the whole of this period.

On a personal level, I sold all my modest portfolio of shares in 2007 as I didn't know how the crisis would play out. This was a good approach as it allowed me to view the credit crunch from the sidelines and avoid the unexpected consequences (banks going bankrupt). Unfortunately although I did buy back into the markets in 2009 I lost my nerve and sold far too early. I had not developed in terms of trading experience and I had not discovered the full Balenthiran Cycle at that point.

Transition from bearish to bullish periods

Conversely during the early days of an economic recovery a long only investor will want to consider moving from being partially invested in the equity markets to being fully invested and investing increasing amounts during the sell offs, thereby holding decreasing amounts of cash. A long and short investor will want to consider closing some short positions and moving from being net short to net long overall.

Again investors need to consider their overall asset allocations and start to reduce their exposure to other asset classes (cash, commodities, bonds, etc.) and use the proceeds to invest in the equity markets. It is best to average in during the final choppy stages of a bear market so that if the market falls further than expected there are more funds available to invest. It is important to realise that valuations often fall to historically low levels during the final stages of a bear market and that cheap shares can often become even cheaper before they start to increase in value.

A buy and hold approach works very well during bull markets but it is always good to take partial profits on investments as the valuations become extreme. Just as cheap shares can become cheaper during a bear market, valuations can continue to rise to extraordinary levels during a bull market so it is advisable to have some continuing exposure to shares that have performed well.

Value shares tend to underperform during a bull market unless they are growing, so growth investing tends to be the best approach for a bull market. The process of investors paying more and more for future earnings growth and expectations growing to unrealistic levels are all part of a bull market and ultimately lead to its demise.

Leverage can be deployed to gain increasing exposure to future gains but this will need to be carefully managed during the early bull market crash and the final collapse. The bull market is expected to last 18 years so investors should make the most of it initially as investments increase in value and economic data starts to confirm the change in trend.

All tools that are available to an investor should be used to provide a performance edge and allow you to fine tune entries and exits, whilst accepting that the precise top or bottom will never be caught. If investing over the whole of the market cycle then it is not necessary to be greedy about the final 10% market move. Looking at 1982 to 2000 as an example, investors could have started to sell after the initial sell off in 1999 at around the 10,500 level on the DJIA, 10% away from the final top. The DJIA was still trading above 11,000 in May 2001 and this would have locked in a gain of more than 10,200 points or 1,300% (from the 1982 low of 776.92) versus a theoretical maximum of 10,996 points.

Technical analysis can be used to identify when the market is overextended and then rolls over on multiple timescales during the year identified by the cycle. The key point is that investors should have a plan in advance of the bull market top or bear market bottom and then they are less likely to succumb to the emotional euphoria or panic that grips the wider public who are uninformed.

The next few years

Applying the Balenthiran Cycle to the current bear market the following clues about the future are revealed – these allow us to plan for the following periods.

2011 to 2013

The model shows that following a high in 2011 the markets will sell off until they reach a low in 2013, although we don't know whether that low will be a lower low or not. It is worth repeating what was said in Chapter 4, under Profile Of A Bear Market: it is important to note that in some cases during the bearish phases, the exact low point may be towards the beginning of that 2.2 year period, but the general negative mood will persist during the whole period. The expectation is that the bear market rally would end in 2011 and from 2011 to 2013 the bear market would continue and it would be a good strategy to take some profits in 2011 and wait for 2013 to reinvest. This should be a significant buying opportunity as the 2013 low should be the last major low of the bear market.

2013 to 2015

Following the low of 2013 there should be a significant rally, however 2015 is not the date of a high, it is when another low is expected. A number of scenarios could emerge; for example, a short fast rally into 2014/15 followed by another bear market or longer rally followed by a quick sell off in 2015. A plan is necessary but it should have some in built flexibility so that it can respond to the unfolding volatile markets. The 2013 low therefore represents a great opportunity to start building long positions for the next 23 years – five remaining years of this bear market and 18 years of the new bull market. If a buy and hold approach from 2013 is to be used then an investment horizon of at least ten years is required, alternatively a trader may wish to take some profits when the markets look overbought with a view to buy back in 2015.

2015

Although not shown in the Balenthiran Cycle, I am forecasting a peak of the secular commodities bull market in 2015. I believe that this is likely to cause the final crisis in the stock bear market and the subsequently deflating commodities bull market will form the basis of the new secular stocks bull market.

2015 to 2018

Another rally is expected but during this period the markets could ultimately move sideways like they did between 1980 and 1982, or they could move significantly higher as they did leading to 1947. The best approach in my opinion is to start stake building following the lows in 2015, and 2013, with the intention of buying great stocks at low valuations and riding the next great bull market. The lows in 2015 and 2018 are likely to be higher lows although I expect to see large percentage falls and continuation of the high volatility that characterises bear markets.

2018 to 2022

The first stage of the new bull market. The move is likely to be dismissed initially by many as just another bear market rally. Falling commodity prices should lead to increasing manufacturing profits as well as increased consumer spending. This is the equivalent of 1982 to 1987 or 1947 to 1950. By 2022 markets should be becoming over-extended and over-hyped. Some profits should be taken at the end of this rally so that they can be reinvested again.

The 2018 to 2053 bull and bear market

The advantage of the Balenthiran Cycle is that it has fixed start and end dates and predetermined intermediate turning points, the cycle can therefore be rolled forward in perpetuity. We are now going to consider the next full cycle – the bull market from 2018 to 2035 and the bear market from 2035 to 2053 – and determine what we can expect along the way.

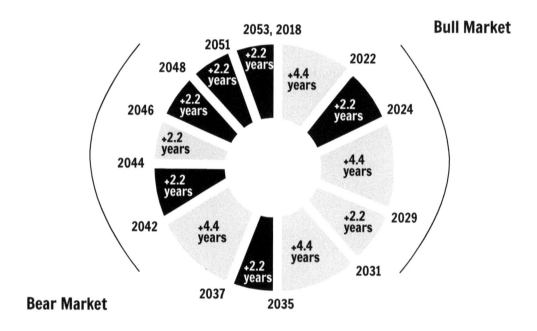

2022 to 2024

A mid-cycle sell off leading to a pause in the bull market. Note that both 1987 and 1950 had swift crashes that were recovered just as swiftly. The market then paused for a few years before resuming its bullish uptrend. If investors had followed the model and bought in 2018, or even 2013 to 2016, then positions should be showing good paper profits and I would be inclined to sit on my hands and do nothing until after a swift move down and use the sell off to add additional long positions. However if there are individual positions that are over-valued then these could be sold leading up to 2022.

2024 to 2035

This is the period where there will be the key upward thrust of the secular bull market. Buy and hold will come back into vogue and a new generation of millions of retail investors will discover the joys of investing in the stock market. A new technological discovery powers a familiar feeling that this time it is different. However it will end in the same way it always does.

2035 to 2053

2035 is the start of a new bear market and by 2035 the DJIA can be expected to have reached the heady levels of 100,000! This seems unbelievable but the rise from 1902 (DJIA 42) to 1929 (DJIA 381) was nine times, the rise from 1942 (DJIA 93) to 1965 (DJIA 969) was ten times and the rise from 1978 (DJIA 908) to 2000 (DJIA 11773) was 13 times. It is not certain where the 2013 low will come but I don't expect to see the levels of 2009.

Taking the average of the magnitude of previous gains (10.6 times) and if it is assumed that there is a low of 9500 in 2013 (a 30% fall from recent highs which is consistent with previous late bear markets), this gives a value of 100,000 for the DJIA in 2035. 2035 will also coincide with the start of a new commodities bull market and that will produce new opportunities for a new generation of investors to switch from equities to commodities and to buy equities during the bear market rallies.

2035 is a long way off and I will be in my early 60s by then. However the usefulness of the Balenthiran Cycle in terms of long-term planning can be seen, as I can plan to reduce my equity holdings as 2035 approaches and move my investments to solid long-term yield-producing assets with few debts and therefore a stable outlook. Property will also be a part of this strategy. The difference between anticipating the end of a secular (or a cyclical) bull market and reacting to the significant crash that follows will make a significant difference to anyone's investment returns and retirement plans.

CHAPTER 6

Conclusion

Nowhere does history indulge in repetitions so often or so uniformly as in Wall Street. When you read contemporary accounts of booms or panics the one thing that strikes you most forcibly is how little either stock speculation or stock speculators today differ from yesterday. The game does not change and neither does human nature.

Jesse Livermore *Reminiscences of a Stock Operator*

Investors are often caught out by changes in sentiment as the stock market represents the collective behaviour of the crowd, and fear and greed tend to lead to exaggerated market movements, booms and busts. It is human nature to look forwards and not backwards, but we know that understanding the past can be insightful in terms of anticipating the future. As human nature does not change, it is likely that behaviour patterns of the past will continue into the future.

We have seen that regular business cycles have been identified by 20th century economists and that cycles of 18 years have featured prominently. We know that studies have confirmed the existence of an alternating 18 year cycle (on average) between stocks and commodities. We have also seen the aspects of human biology that lead to self-reinforcing cycles of boom and bust.

A variety of causes of cycles have been mentioned. This book shows the historic, repetitive pattern that exists in the stock market and extrapolates this into the future. It may be that the human life cycle and demographics are at the heart of cyclical behaviour. Additional cycles such as inventory and credit cycles may develop within the larger cycles and psychology drives these natural trends to extreme levels – booms and busts. Whether this is true or not requires further research and is undoubtedly an incredibly complex field of study which could take a lifetime. In the meantime we have a market roadmap stretching out to 2053. As there are no complex rules that require interpreting, we will be able to measure the accuracy of the Balenthiran Cycle going forwards.

No serious investor can afford to ignore market cycles and, as we have seen, some of the greatest investors consider market cycles as part of their investment approach.

Warren Buffett

Even Warren Buffett, the greatest investor of our time, believes in a 17 year stock market cycle. In an article published in *Fortune* magazine in 1999 which he co-authored Buffett says:

> Now, to get some historical perspective, let's look back at the 34 years before this one—and here we are going to see an almost Biblical kind of symmetry, in the sense of lean years and fat years—to observe what happened in the stock market. Take, to begin with, the first 17 years of the period, from the end of 1964 through 1981. Here's what took place in that interval:
>
> DJIA Dec. 31, 1964: 874.12; Dec. 31, 1981: 875.00
>
> Now I'm known as a long-term investor and a patient guy, but that is not my idea of a big move.[11]

Buffett is known for his fundamental value investment approach analysing individual stocks, he rarely speaks about general stock market levels and doesn't like to forecast where the market may go in the future, in public at least. From this article, however, we have a tantalising glimpse into the fact that Buffett has analysed the past to learn what the future may bring, in terms of general price levels, and he summarised this view as follows:

> Let me summarize what I've been saying about the stock market: I think it's very hard to come up with a persuasive case that equities will over the next 17 years perform anything like—anything like—they've performed in the past 17. If I had to pick the most probable return, from appreciation and dividends combined, that investors in aggregate—repeat, aggregate—would earn in a world of constant interest rates, 2% inflation, and those ever hurtful frictional costs, it would be 6%. If you strip out the inflation component from this nominal return (which you would need to do however inflation fluctuates), that's 4% in real terms. And if 4% is wrong, I believe that the percentage is just as likely to be less as more.[12]

---

[11] http://money.cnn.com/magazines/fortune/fortune_archive/1999/11/22/269071

[12] http://money.cnn.com/magazines/fortune/fortune_archive/1999/11/22/269071

So as the greatest bull market of our generation was heading for a peak, Buffett was warning that this would not continue and the best that we could hope for would be a roughly flat market for the next 17 years.

Buffett attributes this cycle to two factors: interest rates and earnings growth. As we have seen, there are cycles in both credit and commodities that influence interest rates and profits. Buffett also identifies an additional factor.

> These dramatic changes in the two fundamentals that matter most to investors explain much, though not all, of the more than tenfold rise in equity prices—the Dow went from 875 to 9,181— during this 17-year period. What was at work also, of course, was market psychology. Once a bull market gets under way, and once you reach the point where everybody has made money no matter what system he or she followed, a crowd is attracted into the game that is responding not to interest rates and profits but simply to the fact that it seems a mistake to be out of stocks. In effect, these people superimpose an I-can't-miss-the-party factor on top of the fundamental factors that drive the market. Like Pavlov's dog, these "investors" learn that when the bell rings—in this case, the one that opens the New York Stock Exchange at 9:30 a.m.—they get fed. Through this daily reinforcement, they become convinced that there is a God and that He wants them to get rich.

I have described Buffett as the greatest investor of our time because of his consistent ability to grow his funds through many investment cycles avoiding the large draw-downs that cripple countless others; he didn't get lucky from one big bet and then proceed to lose it over the rest of his career. Buffett's study of market history, market psychology and the fact that the same investment mistakes and misallocation of capital happen over and over again has arguably played as important a role as fundamental analysis in growing, and more importantly preserving, his fortune over his lifetime. Perhaps giving him the confidence to maintain his contrarian position when he was slightly early with his prognosis, despite public ridicule and temporary sub-par investment returns.

The importance of timing

Stock market bubbles show us that investors are full of enthusiasm for stocks at precisely the wrong time and conversely they are repulsed by stocks when they represent their best value from a price-earnings perspective. The majority of investors have a tendency to extrapolate the recent past into the future and expect that this trend will continue indefinitely. This is why timing is so important – we need to have the right strategy for current market conditions but also anticipate when the current cycle is coming to an end and act accordingly.

One of the problems that people have with cycles is that they can't agree on the starting point, the ending point or the duration of the cycle. There are numerous articles about 10 year, 12 year, 14 year and 16 year bull markets beginning at various points in history. It stands to reason that if we cannot get agreement on these basic aspects of a cycle then it should be questioned whether the cycle actually exists at all.

I have tried to tackle this head on by not only being clear about definitive start and end points but also having a specific duration and demonstrating how the cycle repeats over 100 years. For a cycle to be valid it should work now and it should work when extrapolated backwards to the early days of the stock market. If this works then we can have a high degree of confidence in extrapolating it forwards into the future.

The 17 year stock market cycle that Buffett describes has been identified by others as well. In *Anatomy of the Bear* Russell Napier writes:

> According to Professor Jeremy Siegel's analysis of total returns since 1802, all an investor needs to do is hold for 17 years and they will never lose money in the stock market. If you sit it out and ignore market prices, history suggests that in sometime less than 17 years the bear will simply go away, leaving your real purchasing power undamaged.[13]

This book identifies when the start of the 17.6 year period is and when investors should position themselves for the next great bull market. We have seen how the Balenthiran Cycle identifies not only the start and end dates of bull and bear markets, but also the intermediate high and low turning points, providing investors with a critical edge in terms of market timing.

---

[13] *Anatomy of the Bear*, Russell Napier.

Are your eyes open or shut?

In 2013 we are likely to see a significant bear market low that will provide a great opportunity to buy stocks which will then progress through a twice in a lifetime bull market lasting until 2035.

The low in 2013 will not be the end of the bear market and I expect to see another low in 2015. But I believe that 2013 will mark the last significant low of the bear market and we should see higher highs and higher lows after that point.

This bear market is well advanced in terms of stocks, property is still far too expensive in many parts of the world based on historic valuations (such as incomes), the commodity cycle is approaching the end and bonds (arguably the next bubble to burst) are where most money managers have parked their money due to the ongoing economic uncertainty. 2013 provides an unparalleled opportunity to get back into the stock market and to ride the new bull market. We need to be patient and take a five year view before we start to see the fruits of that investment strategy but the bull market will follow, as sure as day follows night. When the wall of money that is invested in government bonds starts to move we will see some major market shifts. There has not been a blow-off top in commodities with wide market participation and I believe that is yet to come. That is consistent with the Balenthiran Cycle view that the start of a new equity bull market is a few years away.

This means that a glorious period for a stock market investor is about to begin. It may not feel like it now, and I'm sure it didn't feel like it in the early 1980s or the mid 1940s, but that's what the cycle is telling us. Common sense says that this period of credit tightening and sovereign debt worries won't last forever.

But when will it end?

The Balenthiran Cycle says this bear market will end in 2018.

Whatever you think about the existence of cycles and what causes them, it is hard to argue with the facts presented in this book. There is a saying that only monkeys pick bottoms and the Balenthiran Cycle is primarily intended to show changes in bullish and bearish sentiment; however it regularly identifies the specific year of a market turning point. The Balenthiran Cycle cannot be relied upon on its own and investors still need to apply individual investment skills. There is no guarantee that this cycle will continue into the future; markets are unpredictable and investors need to ensure that risk is managed as it always should be.

Many people will also take exception to the argument that market forces are predetermined and that individuals have no input or control over the future. However I am not suggesting that things are predetermined. What I am presenting can be thought of as a stock market growth cycle similar to that of human beings. Distinct phases exist such as baby, infant, child, teenager, adult, middle aged, old aged. These are predetermined, nothing you do will change the fact that these stages will occur. Of course the decisions that you make daily will determine the quality of your life during these phases and if you succeed and achieve a prosperous life you may also prolong the later stages through healthy eating and living and mental well being. And so it is with the stock market. What you actually take away from it will depend on your individual decisions and what you learn along the way. The market's framework is defined and cyclical, but you make your choices with either your eyes open or shut.

APPENDICES

HOW I DISCOVERED THE 17.6 YEAR STOCK MARKET CYCLE

Observation, experience, memory and mathematics - these are what the successful trader must depend on.

Jesse Livermore *Reminiscences of a Stock Operator*

When I first started to research market cycles my immediate thought was that if I could discover the cause of market cycles then I would be able to determine the cycle length and thereby prove the existence of a specific market cycle. Cycles exist in many areas of nature and even if it was as simple as the weather influencing crop yields which in turn affects disposable incomes, a natural cycle impacting the stock market seemed like the most likely. However this proved to be a frustrating and ultimately unsuccessful approach. The possibilities are endless and nothing I tried provided a consistent cycle that could be extrapolated backwards to the early 20th century.

While reading a book on mathematicians I came across Pythagoras and his assertion that "all is number". Pythagoras believed that numbers held special significance and that the relationship between numbers could be found all around us, from the movement of the planets to musical harmony. It was at this point that I started to focus on the actual movement of the DJIA and empirical observation of the changes in bullish and bearish sentiment in the stock market.

I studied mathematics at university and one of the books I read was about famous mathematicians throughout history and their effect on modern life. Pythagoras and Fibonacci were two of the mathematicians mentioned and I will discuss them briefly because their ideas shaped my thinking. I am only going to cover the concepts that permeated my subconscious and which are related to the discovery of the Balenthiran Cycle.

Pythagoras

Pythagoras was a philosopher in ancient Greece (born around 570 BC) and is famous for the theorem that bears his name. He believed that 10 was the most special number as it was the sum of the first four integers which also represented the elements; earth, air, fire and water (1+2+3+4=10). The number 10 also formed the perfect triangle as symbolised by the tetractys below:

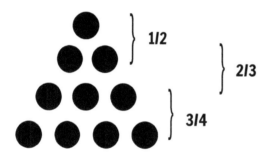

The first row represents a point (zero dimension), the second row a line (one dimension), the third row a triangle (two dimensions) and the fourth row represents a tetrahedron (a three dimensional pyramid representing three dimensions).

Pythagoras also discovered that when the ratios of the tetractys 1:2, 2:3 and 3:4 were applied to string lengths they produced sounds that were pleasing to the ear. 1:2 is an octave, 2:3 is a perfect fifth and 3:4 is a perfect fourth.

I wondered whether there are naturally occurring mathematical relationships in terms of stock market cycles, for example whether cyclical bear markets, which are always shorter than cyclical bull markets, are half or two-thirds the length of a bull market.

Fibonacci

Fibonacci was an Italian mathematician (born around 1170) who introduced the West to the sequence that is obtained by starting with 0 and then 1 and adding the previous two numbers together to get the next number in the sequence as follows:

0, 1, 1, 2, 3, 5, 8, 13, 21, 34, 55, 89, 144, 233, 377, 610, 987.....................................

As well as being the solution to a problem involving the idealised growth of rabbit populations, the higher up the sequence, the closer two consecutive Fibonacci numbers when divided by each other get to the *golden ratio* (1:1.618 or 0.618:1).

The golden ratio is found in many areas of nature and is commonly used by traders in order to forecast how far a market will retrace before continuing in its primary direction.

Once again here is a mathematical concept that can be seen in the world around us. For example, the golden ratio can be found in the way that leaves are arranged around the stem of a plant so that the plant will be exposed to the optimal amount of light and rain (i.e. without the leaves blocking each other).

It could be a coincidence that these mathematical concepts of Pythagoras and Fibonacci are also naturally occurring phenomena but this reinforced my belief that these ideas could be applied to stock market cycles. While researching I came across the work of William Gann, who also believed that mathematical patterns existed in the stock market.

Gann

W. D. Gann was an American investor (born in 1878) who noticed relationships in stock market trends based upon the ratios 1:2, 1:3, 1:4, 1:8 1:16.....

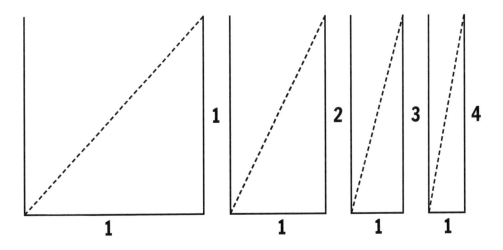

Gann used these lines on stock charts as an early form of technical analysis to predict where the price would go in the future and together the lines are commonly referred to as a Gann fan.

It was at this at this point, incorporating the ideas of Pythagoras, Fibonacci and Gann, that I started to look for mathematical relationships in the markets. Cycles that could be subdivided by 2, 3, 4, etc., and also multiplied by 2, 3, 4, etc., to arrive at smaller sub-cycles and larger cycles respectively.

18 Year Cycle

As mentioned in Chapter 1, 18 years is a commonly quoted cycle for both the commodity markets and stock market. I knew that this was an approximate length as this did not extrapolate backwards exactly – but 18 years was a starting point.

I noted that the factors of 18 (numbers that can be divided into 18) are 1, 2, 3, 6, 9, 18 and that 18 divides quite neatly in terms of the ratios of the Fibonacci sequence:

	1	2	3	5	8
18 divided by	18	9	6	3.6	2.25

Eureka, despair, joy

The next step was to design a model that would allow me to input the first order cycle (an initial cycle of, for example, two years or three years, where the larger secular cycle is a multiple of this initial cycle) and this would apply the cycle backwards over the previous 100 years, starting at 2000, and identify turning points back to 1900 and forwards to 2100.

Through a process of trial and error I was able to determine that the first order cycle was 2.2 years long. 2.2 years matched important market turning points such as 1929, 1987, 2000 and 2007. Although there were in fact many more turning points given by the 2.2 year cycle than actually occurred, I realised that this was an important breakthrough as I had not previously managed to include both 1929 and 1987 with 2000 in a cycle before. The actual process of discovery was not as simple as described here. There were numerous false starts and periods where I abandoned my research for months before returning to it with a fresh mind.

Further observation of the dates provided by the 2.2 year cycle, and linking with the ideas of Gann, showed that the bull cycle was twice the length of the bear cycle, i.e. the bull cycle length is 4.4 years and the bear cycle length is 2.2 years. Continued development led to the 17.6 year cycle and the Balenthiran Cycle Model.

It was at this point, after I amalgamated the 4.4 year and 2.2 year cycles into the 17.6 year cycle, that I entered "17.6 year stock market cycle" into a search engine to see if anything had been written about it. I was honestly not expecting anything to come up, as 17.6 years is very specific. Disappointed doesn't begin to describe how I felt when I saw that not only had Art Cashin beaten me to it, but that he had discussed the 17.6 year cycle on CNBC! As I watched a clip of the interview, however, it very quickly dawned on me that far from being a negative, this was in fact hugely positive. Firstly, if the cycle exists then it is reasonable to assume that other people have identified it. Secondly, Cashin has already introduced the concept of a cycle of length 17.6 years to America, or at least to those who watch CNBC.

Alignment with other cycles

I was also struck by the fact that the Balenthiran 17.6 year stock market cycle fits in with multiples of some of the smaller cycles previously identified in Chapter 2. For example:

- 4 x 17.6 years = 70.4 years (Elliott Supercycle)

- 3 x 17.6 years = 52.8 years (Kondratieff Wave)

- 2 x 17.6 years = 35.2 years (full stock market cycle, trough to trough or peak to peak)

- 17.6 years (Balenthiran Cycle)

- 17.6 years ÷ 2 = 8.8 years (Juglar Cycle)

- 17.6 years ÷ 4 = 4.4 years (Kitchin Cycle)

- 8.8 years ÷ 3 = 2.93 years (Mills Cycle)

Theory first then proof

While some may deride observation as a legitimate scientific method, there are numerous cases in history where scientists observed a phenomenon and developed a theory, which remained a theory for many years until it was proved conclusively. The most recent example is the discovery of the Higgs bosen particle; and arguably the most important of all was that the Sun and not the Earth is the centre of the solar system.

Modern economic theory is just that – a theory, based on the ideas of rational decision making by unemotional human beings. However the natural human instinct when under stress is towards fight or flight. For a great many investors, faced with the prospect of losing a large amount of their capital during a crisis, the rational decision is flight. Too much emphasis was placed on the potential of outsized rewards, the downside risks were either not explained or not fully understood, therefore when an investment doesn't perform as expected then that is a lesson learned and they promptly sell.

As we have seen, this boom and bust cycle has occurred throughout history and will continue in the future for as long as humans are involved in markets. The Balenthiran Cycle is also a theory, based on human nature and the human life cycle. The test of my theory will come in its ability to accurately forecast future stock market trends.

BIBLIOGRAPHY

The Alchemy of Finance: Reading the Mind of the Market, George Soros

Anatomy of the Bear: Lessons from Wall Street's Four Great Bottoms, Russell Napier

Boom Bust: House Prices, Banking and the Depression of 2010, Fred Harrison

Business Cycles: A Theoretical, Historical and Statistical Analysis of the Capitalist Process, Rendigs Fels & Joseph A. Schumpeter

Elliott Wave Principle: Key to Market Behavior, A. J. Frost and Robert Prechter

The Great Depression Ahead: How to Prosper in the Crash Following the Greatest Boom in History, Harry S. Dent

The Great Super Cycle: Profit from the Coming Inflation Tidal Wave and Dollar Devaluation, David Skarica

Hot Commodities: How Anyone Can Invest Profitably in the World's Best Market, Jim Rogers

Introducing Economics: A Graphic Guide, David Orrell & Borin Van Loon

The New Paradigm For Financial Markets: The Credit Crisis of 2008 and What It Means, George Soros

Reminiscences Of A Stock Operator, Edwin Lefèvre

Stock Trader's Almanac 2012, Jeffrey A. Hirsch and Yale Hirsch

SuperCycles: The New Economic Force Transforming Global Markets and Investment Strategy, Arun Motianey

INDEX

eBook edition

As a buyer of the print edition of *The 17.6 Year Stock Market Cycle* you can now download the eBook edition free of charge to read on an eBook reader, your smartphone or your computer. Go to:

http://ebooks.harriman-house.com/stockmarketcycle

or point your smartphone at the QRC below.

You can then register and download your free eBook.

www.harriman-house.com

 Harriman House

www.ingramcontent.com/pod-product-compliance
Ingram Content Group UK Ltd.
Pitfield, Milton Keynes, MK11 3LW, UK
UKHW030737291224
452885UK00006B/64